Piglets vs. Pugs

★ Julie Beer ★

NATIONAL
GEOGRAPHIC
KiDS

Washington, D.C.

Contents

Before they assume their battle stations, let's check in with the competitors!

PIGLET

Pitter-pattering in on all fours is that cutie patootie we all know as Piglet! Her scientific name may be *Sus scrofa domesticus*, but don't even think about calling her scruffy! Domestic pigs may have a reputation for being dirty, but that's just trash talk. They are actually quite clean animals. OK, sure, they do roll in the mud from time to time—but that doesn't mean we can't have a good, clean fight!

FYI: We say piglet everywhere, but sometimes we just show pictures of a pig— a grown-up piglet. They're just so darn cute, too!

PUG

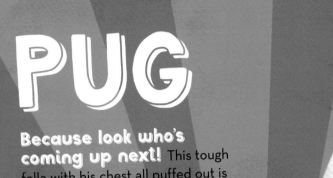

Because look who's coming up next! This tough fella with his chest all puffed out is the incomparable Pug! Boy, this guy sure looks ... um ... fierce? Ferocious? All right, all right, he's ridiculously cute! Pugs are officially members of *Canis lupus familiaris*, that big ole group that all domestic dogs belong to. But this is no status quo pup—this is a champ in the making! Can he clean up like Piglet? Or better yet, can Pug wipe the floor with Piglet in this competition?

Well, there you have it folks—this is going to be one close competition. Either Piglet or Pug could win this one by a nose ... er ... snout. What it really comes down to is who YOU think is going to win this matchup. Are you going to put your paws in the air like you just don't care and vote for Team Pug? Or are you going to go big and land on Team Pig? The good news is you don't have to decide just yet. In fact, wait a little bit and weigh your options. There's a lot to learn about these two competitors, including some little-known facts that may surprise you. So curl up like a pig's (or pug's!) tail with this book and let the throwdown begin!

Wildest at Heart

Before we roll up our sleeves and do some serious comparing of how pigs and pugs measure up today, let's take a quick peek into their pasts—the roots that got them to where they are. Prior to being domestic pigs living on farms—and even pets brought into homes—pigs were wild hogs living in forests looking for snacks. Pugs, on the other hand, sat on the laps of kings.

Time-out for a fast fact: 2,500 YEARS AGO, PUGS WERE KEPT AS PETS AT BUDDHIST MONASTERIES.

Pugs

Somewhere around 40,000 years ago, dogs separated from their family line of wolves and eventually became the lovable, huggable pups we know today. At first, dogs were taught to hunt, herd sheep, and protect flocks from predators. Some were kept to guard homes. Others were bred specifically to be friends to humans. It's no surprise what the best fit was for pugs. Yep, Pug was humankind's bestie from the get-go. Pugs are one of the oldest breeds of dogs, likely getting their start in Tibet about 2,500 years ago and then spreading to Japan and Europe. Popular because of their small size and big personality, pugs became a favorite with royal families in Holland, especially after one pug in the 16th century was said to have saved a prince's life by waking him up when Spanish invaders tried to attack him in his sleep. Super Pug to the rescue!

Piglets

Pooches had long been lapdogs by the time humans got around to domesticating wild boars. About 9,000 years ago, boars were corralled in the Middle East and China and bred to be the tame domestic oinkers they are today. Explorers and settlers brought these domesticated pigs with them on ships to North and South America and Australia. While pigs lagged behind dogs when it came to hanging out with humans as pets, they were one of the first farmyard animals to be domesticated. Today there are about one billion domestic pigs in the world, and countless wild hogs. (Domestic pigs tend to be bigger and less hairy than wild ones.) While dogs beat out domestic pigs in a contest of "who came first," these days, the world population of domestic pigs outnumbers that of dogs two to one.

All hail the royal pugness!

11

Most Likely to Tip the Scales

Like all serious fights, this one begins with a weigh-in. We all know that bigger doesn't always mean better, but boy, does Piglet have a hoof up in this category. But don't worry Pug fans—some of the greatest Olympic athletes are small but mighty. If Pug is the Simone Biles of this competition, he has nothing to worry about!

Piglets

This little piggy isn't so little!

Pigs come in all shapes and sizes, but when they're born, domestic piglets typically weigh about 2.5 pounds (1.1 kg). However, you can only call them itty-bitty for a few days. They double their weight in their first week! By the time they're full-grown, domestic pigs can easily tip the scales at a hefty 300-700 pounds (136-318 kg). A pig named Big Norm from New York, U.S.A., weighed a whopping 1,600 pounds (726 kg) and was dubbed the world's heaviest pig. Potbellied pigs, bred from domestic Vietnamese breeds, sometimes go by the nickname "teacup pigs," but they can't fit in a teacup for long! They grow up to be 100-175 pounds (45-79 kg), on average—about the weight of a Saint Bernard. But they're only about two feet (0.6 m) tall. So "teapot" might really be a better name for potbellies—short and stout!

Time-out for a fast fact:
A FULL-GROWN DOMESTIC PIG CAN WEIGH AS MUCH AS A GRAND PIANO.

Pugs

Oh, little Pug. His chunky build doesn't scream lightweight, but compared to Piglet, he's, well, just a little bug. When he is eight weeks old, a pug is about the same size as a newborn piglet. But that's where the growth comparison ends. Full-grown pugs grow to an average of 14–18 pounds (6–8 kg) and are a mere 10–14 inches (25–36 cm) from paw to shoulder. But be warned, Piglet: Pugs are associated with the Latin phrase *multum in parvo*, meaning "a lot in a small space." Small and powerful? Don't underestimate Pug just yet!

Biggest Smarty-Pants

Sit, stay, shake, fetch ... A dog like Pug can understand as many as 150 commands and words, but there's more to smarts than just words. Pigs are excellent problem-solvers and have been known to figure out simple puzzles. So who's going to outsmart whom in this battle of wits?

Pugs

OK, it's true—tongue out and drooling is not the best way to show up to an IQ test. But keep in mind, dogs have different types of smarts. In the 1990s, a canine psychologist described intelligence as being divided into different categories. He defined "instinctive intelligence" as what a dog is bred to be good at: For example, retrievers, including Labrador retrievers, are naturally good at fetching. "Adaptive intelligence" is a measure of how good a dog is at figuring things out—like problem-solving. "Working intelligence" is how good a dog is at following orders. During his research, he surveyed 199 dog obedience judges to rank more than 140 breeds in these areas of intelligence. Pugs ranked 110th. Ouch! (Border collies, poodles, and German shepherds claimed the top three positions.) Poor Pug! But the judges noted there are always individual exceptions within a breed. Pugs' strength? Learning new tricks. These natural clowns can easily be taught to shake, play dead, and even jump through Hula-Hoops—especially for a treat.

Piglets

Pigs might not be known for giving high fives, but they have some other tricks up their sleeves. In 2009, a team of researchers found that pigs can easily learn tasks, like operating levers to get food. Other studies show they can work together to solve problems—putting them on par with dolphins and chimps in terms of intelligence. Ever catch your pooch staring at him or herself in the mirror? It's likely your pup doesn't actually know what he or she is looking at. But there's a chance pigs might. In another 2009 study, a group of pigs was able to locate a hidden bowl of food using mirrors. Sorry, Pug, but Piglet might just be the fairest of them all.

Biggest Foodie

Now here's a subject near and dear to both Piglet's and Pug's mouth ... er, heart. Food! There may be nothing more important to either one of them than a tasty little morsel. It's time to see which one will win this epic food fight!

Piglets

Whoa there, Piglet. You're eating like, well, a pig! There's a reason pigs have a reputation for being such food hogs. They sure can chow down! Pigs are also omnivores. That means that in the wild they eat everything from worms to grasses to acorns to insects to eggs—even young birds and reptiles. Domestic pigs, especially ones kept as pets, do some rooting around for food, but their main meal source is special pig feed, which is made from a mix of grains that includes corn, oats, and soybean meal. They generally eat 1 to 2 percent of their overall body weight in pig feed every day. That's not to say the occasional treat—for pigs that's some fresh veggies—isn't also appreciated!

Time-out for a fast fact: PIGS KEPT INDOORS AS PETS HAVE BEEN KNOWN TO FIGURE OUT HOW TO OPEN A FRIDGE AND FORAGE FOR THEIR OWN SNACKS!

Pugs

Since we all know that dogs are constantly eating homework, you can bet pugs enjoy their fair share of snacks. Look at those eyes—they definitely say "Feed me." Which means pugs are prone to getting a little chunky around the middle. The best food for pugs is good old dry dog chow—usually made from chicken, grain, and added vitamins and minerals—and split into two servings of about a half cup each during the day. And there are a few human foods that are no-no's for all dogs, including chocolate, cinnamon, garlic, onions, ice cream, and almonds. Since they are small dogs to begin with, even a few extra snacks can add up quickly, which veterinarians say isn't good for their overall health. So while Pug may be perfectly masterful at munching, in this food fight, it might be wise that he not pig out!

This competition is bananas!

Most Likely to Be a Track Star

Let's put this delicately: Neither pugs nor pigs are exactly built for speed. But if they were put to a race, which one would cross the finish line first?

Pugs

Pugs are good for a quick sprint to chase a ball, and boy, do they come running when dinner's ready. But if you want to take a dog out with you for a nice long run, Pug's not your guy. Those little legs weren't meant to go the distance! Pugs do need some exercise in order to stay fit and trim, but unlike high-energy breeds, like border collies and poodles, pugs aren't chomping at the bit for more. After a quick romp, Pug is more than happy to settle in and chill.

Piglets

Piglet doesn't look like much of an all-star athlete, but put her in a race and she can probably outrun you! Adult domestic pigs can run at speeds up to 11 miles an hour (18 km/h)—that's a 5.5-minute mile (1.6 km)! In fact, some county fairs in the United States have pig racing competitions, in which the oinkers speed around a track. What's a pig's motivation to be the leader of the pack? The cookie at the end, of course.

Time-out for a fast fact: PIGS HAVE NOTHING ON THEIR WILD ANCESTORS—WILD BOARS CAN SPRINT UP TO 30 MILES AN HOUR (48 KM/H) AND CAN JUMP A THREE-FOOT (1-M)-TALL FENCE!

19

Stranger Superstition

It's probably pretty safe for a pug to cross your path, but there are times when pooches don't bring the best of fortune. Pigs also can come with mixed blessings. Let's see if Piglet or Pug has the better luck at winning this battle!

Pugs

Pugs aren't generally big barkers, but plenty of their canine relatives are, which has given dogs an association with spooky superstition. One common association is that of a howling dog at night being an omen of death. This can be traced back to ancient Egypt—the god who took care of the dead was Anubis, who had the head of a jackal—which is in the same family as dogs. A howling dog was seen as calling a soul to Anubis. Today, some pugs are good luck charms. When the University of Southern California (USC) men's basketball team needed some good luck to get into the 2017 NCAA tournament, they turned to a pug. The USC coach credited his pug puppy Cali with helping the team make the cut. Cali appeared at a press conference before the tournament started sporting her USC sweater, and then cheered from her home when her team made it to the second round of March Madness.

Piglets

In Ireland and China, pigs are a symbol of good luck. In fact, the pig is the 12th animal in the 12-year cycle of the Chinese zodiac. (Every 12 years is the Year of the Pig.) But don't get all high-and-mighty, Piglet! Guess what animal occupies the 11th position of the Chinese zodiac? The dog! In the late 19th and early 20th centuries, pigs also were particularly popular in Europe because having a lot of them was a sign of wealth and prosperity. People carried charms shaped like pigs for good luck. And pigs may bring a warning of bad weather: An old superstition says that when pigs run with straw in their mouths, a storm or high winds are coming.

Time-out for a fast fact: A NORSE LEGEND TELLS OF THE GODDESS FREYJA, WHO WAS IN CHARGE OF DEATH, AMONG OTHER THINGS, AND RODE A CHARIOT PULLED BY GIANT CATS. BECAUSE DOGS AND CATS ARE NATURAL ENEMIES, PEOPLE BELIEVED THAT WHEN DEATH (FREYJA) WAS COMING, DOGS WOULD HOWL.

Curliest Tail

Maybe what this battle is going to come down to isn't Pug and Piglet's differences, but rather how they are most alike. And for this category, if you were to flip a coin to determine the winner, it would most certainly come up tails!

Pugs

Besides his squishy nose and bulgy eyes, Pug's defining characteristic is a corkscrew tail. All full-grown purebred pugs have a curly tail that tucks up over one hip, unless there has been an injury, causing it to straighten out. And if you want to get extra fancy, about 25 percent of registered purebred pugs have double curls—two loops! But baby pugs are known to let their hair down from time to time: When a puppy pug sleeps or is relaxed, its tail will sometimes uncurl.

Time-out for a fast fact:
MOST PUPPIES DON'T WAG THEIR TAIL UNTIL THEY ARE AROUND SIX WEEKS OLD.

Piglets

Watch out, Pug! Piglet is right on your tail! That quintessential curlicue is what you think of on every farmyard pig, but not every pig's tail curls. Wild boars have straight tails. And the tails of those adorable potbellied pigs? Straight as a pencil. Domestic pigs have curly tails, and if you look carefully, this can tell a lot about a pig's mood. A straight tail on a curly-tailed pig means the pig is feeling defensive, a gentle wagging tail means it is relaxed, and a twitchy tail means it is stressed or fearful. Boy, it sure is hard to make heads or tails of this battle!

Is anyone else's head spinning in circles?

Biggest All-Star

It looks like it's time to get serious and see which has more muscle in this matchup. Let's take a look at some pigs and pugs that are gold medal worthy.

Piglets

A pig surfing the waves of Oahu, Hawaii, U.S.A.?

You might say, "Give me a *break!*" But believe it or not, it's true. Kama heads out to the sea with his owner, Kai Holt, and walks right up to the end of the surfboard to catch a wave while Kai steers. Kama's stocky build helps him keep steady on the board. And when he falls off? He goes wee, wee, wee, swimming all the way back to the board. Surfing appears to run in Kama's family: Kama's son and granddaughter piglets also hang ten! (Or should we say, hang hooves?) Hopefully, Pug doesn't wipe out in this competition!

And the winner is ... Pug!

That's what the announcers said in 1981, when Dhandy's Favorite Woodchuck—better known as Chucky—won Best in Show at the Westminster Kennel Club Dog Show, the only time to date a pug has won the top prize in the competition. Out of the 2,910 dogs in the prestigious contest, Chucky came out number one. The judge of the final round said the pug had "that extra little spark of animation and showmanship that put him over the top."

Cutest Baby

Whoa! Talk about an even matchup! I've gone back and forth so many times during this battle I'm seeing double!

I couldn't agree more, Bob. How about we take a breather for a moment and turn things over to our special correspondent, Franco. He's going to take us back to a time when Pug and Piglet were little tots.

Thanks, Peggy! Brace yourself for cuteness overload because things are about to get adorable in here! We know that pigs have super smarts, but did you know that learning starts right out of the gate? Newborn piglets learn their name by the time they are two weeks old and come running when they hear their mother's call.

Well, that's simply darling.

Oh, I'm just getting started. Mother pigs sing to their piglets while they eat! And when the little piggies aren't stuffing their faces, they might give their mom a little snuggle by rubbing their snouts on her face. Piglets also enjoy a romp from time to time. They like to hop and jump, often carry around sticks, and even play chase with their siblings. A favorite pig game is to toss straw in the air! Studies have shown that pigs are at their most playful when they are just wee little ones. They reach their play-ful peak between the ages of 6 and 14 weeks. And if you think that's cute, here's the cherry on top: Pigs love close contact with each other. When they take a nap, they often sleep nose to nose.

What?! A piggy cuddle puddle?! Oh, Pug, how are you going to top this?

It won't be easy. But here's a riddle for you: What's cuter than a pug?

OK, you got me. What?

A half dozen pug puppies! A mama pug averages four to six puppies in her litter. Picture this: A newborn pug is so small it can fit in your hand. Like all dogs, pugs are born with their eyes closed, but within a few weeks, they open. It's just as well those eyes are closed—a pug snoozes 22 hours a day for its first few weeks of life! The other two hours are entirely focused on eating. Pugs generally weigh less than a pound (454 g) when born, but before you know it, they are up and about and ready to play with their brothers and sisters. Favorite activities by six weeks old are rolling around and nibbling on each other. Pugs aren't ready to be adopted, though, until they are about two months old.

I just want to give that pug a hug.

No time for cuddles, Peggy! We have a funny face-off to get back to! Put your game face back on, Pug and Piglet. Back to the battle!

27

Biggest Celebrity

Pardon *moi*? Could there be a bigger star than Missy Piggy? Well, better watch out, diva! There's one pug out there that may outshine even you!

Piglets

Not only does Miss Piggy rub elbows with famous frogs, her film and TV career has never waned. Plus, she has tens of thousands of followers on Twitter! She'd never admit it, but Miss Piggy is just one of numerous celebrity pigs: There's Wilbur, the lovable pig of *Charlotte's Web*; Winnie the Pooh's buddy Piglet; Babe, from the movie of the same name; Hamm from *Toy Story* ... and let us not forget the Three Little Pigs. Think you can huff and puff and blow Piglet out of this race, Pug?

Pugs

Three words: Doug the Pug. Nicknamed the king of pop culture, Doug has eight million followers across his social media accounts. He also has a best-selling book, was featured in a music video, and has an online store that features everything from ugly "pugly" sweat-shirts to look-alike Doug the Pug plush stuffies. Sure, Miss Piggy is chummy with Kermit and Fozzie, but Doug has hung out with Ed Sheeran. And when he isn't hanging out with celebs, he's imper-sonating them—from Moana to One Direction—in his online videos.

Best Peepers

I spy a tight competition! This category may be a duel over best vision, but both Pug and Piglet have their eyes on the prize: winning this historic battle!

Piglets

Pigs lead with their snout, not with their eyes. Even though they have a 310-degree panoramic view of the world, their small, bleary eyes are a giveaway of their poor vision. And because the world isn't in focus, pigs tend to be cautious of new places and they startle easy. To top it off, their night vision is even worse. Pigs, however, do have limited color vision. They don't see as many colors as people do, but they can tell the difference between colors. Alas, the outlook for Piglet winning this category is pretty blurry!

Pugs

Bulgy eyes are one of Pug's most distinct trademarks. But they come with a few drawbacks. Because they stick out more than a typical dog's eyes, they are more likely to get scratched and are easily irritated. Like all dogs, Pug sees the world in a less colorful way than humans do. In fact, red is just a shade of brownish gray to him. Doggy Christmas sweaters aren't nearly as festive through a pug's peepers! Even though Pug's eyes are a little high maintenance, his vision is like a hawk's compared to poor Piglet's. Pug wins this category with a knockout, and Piglet is seeing stars!

31

Best
Dressed

It looks like Piglet and Pug are all dressed up and ready to step into the photo booth! Which will get the most likes? Check out these selfies to decide which wins best dressed.

#RunwayReady
I'M SOW READY TO STRUT MY STUFF!

#It'sMyBoarDay
I'LL SQUEAL IF I WANT TO!

#LePIGchaun
KISS ME. I'M IRISH!

#TheManeEvent
I DON'T HAVE TOO MUCH PRIDE TO WEAR THIS COSTUME!

#RoyalRoots
I'M DEFINITELY RULING THIS OUTFIT.

#WigOut
HAIR TODAY, GONE TOMORROW!

#CountPUGula
TOO CUTE TO BE SCARY.

Best Moniker

This battle is so tight that both Pug and Piglet could sure use a little bump right about now to get ahead. Walking away with the best nickname might give one of them the edge to gain an all-new title: Winner.

Pugs

All pug owners have a nickname for their little puggly wugglys—maybe it's snuggle puggle or buggy puggy. But have you stopped and wondered how pugs first got their name? It has to do with that cute mug, of course. It is believed that because a pug's facial expression is similar to a marmoset monkey's, a popular pet in the 1700s that was known as a "pug," the name was transferred to the pooch. In Germany, though, pugs aren't pugs—they're called mops!

Time-out for a fast fact: A GROUP OF PUGS IS CALLED A GRUMBLE.

34

Piglets

OK, Piglet. What can you bring to this battle of the nickname? Can you top Mops? Well, there's the obvious "piggy," and the occasional "oinker." But here's something you might not know: While a group of pigs is usually called a herd, its traditional name is a drift. And a group of wild pigs was once called a sounder. And let us not forget pot-bellied pigs! That droopy round belly gave them their adorable nickname. Still, when it comes to clever and sweet, Mops might have just mopped up this category, Piglet!

Greatest Groomer

For a gal that likes to unwind in a mud bath, you'd think Piglet would be bumped from winning this category faster than Pug could spell groomer. But don't give the win to Pug just yet: Piglet may just be more squeaky-clean than you think.

Sure, she lives in a pig-pen full of mud ... that she wallows in. But don't be so quick to judge! Piglet has a very sensible reason for those mud baths: Mud keeps her cool. Pigs don't have functional sweat glands (that whole "sweat like a pig" saying is hogwash!), so hanging out in mud keeps them comfortable on hot days. It also keeps mosquitoes away. A group of wild boars in Switzerland were particularly tidy: When they were given apples covered in sand, instead of eating them, they carried them to a creek, pushed them around in the water with their snouts, and ate them after they were clean!

Time-out for a fast fact:
PIGS CAN GET SUNBURNS JUST LIKE PEOPLE. A LAYER OF MUD ACTS LIKE SUNSCREEN.

Pug may not be the perfect roommate—water bowl spills just come with the territory—but he's a pretty tidy guy. He sheds a little, but he's no golden retriever. However, pugs do have a bit of a reputation with ... now this is a little personal ... passing gas. Yep, everyone toots, including Pug. Maybe even a little more than other dogs. Pugs are known for being gassy for a few reasons. Pugs (along with boxers, Boston terriers, and bulldogs) are brachycephalic, which means they have a short, broad skull. This makes it harder for them to pick up kibble out of their bowl, and because of the shape of their snout, they gobble up a bunch of food at once—causing them to also gulp down air. Which eventually makes them, well, gassy.

Was that you, Pug?

Biggest Loudmouth

Maybe the winner of this competition is going to be the one who can grab the most attention. Let's see which one is the bigger noisemaker.

Piglets

Imagine how loud a chain saw is. It's cover-your-ears-with-your-hands loud, right? Well, that is exactly how loud a pig's squeal is. Ranging between 110 and 115 decibels, a pig's squeal is loud enough to be considered dangerous if you listen to it for more than a minute straight on a regular basis. A pig is so loud it should come with a warning label!

Hmm, I don't know if I'd want to be the winner of this category!

Pugs

A barking pug may cause an eye roll, but rarely is it ear-piercing. Pugs aren't known for their intimidating woof, although barking is one of the ways pugs communicate—especially if they want attention. There is one time pugs are especially noisy—when they're sleeping! They are notorious snorers. These snoozing sounds are common in pugs because of the structure of their snout. That short snout is cause for serious loud slumbers. Even so, Pug, in this category you're going to need to put on some earmuffs because Piglet knows how to turn up the volume!

Most Laid-back

Nap time! Pugs spend about 14 hours a day snoozing. Those little lap-warmers need their beauty rest! And being aggressive just isn't Pug's vibe. Pigs, on the other hand, can get a little territorial. And they sleep less than eight hours a day. That's less sleep than you get! Does that mean Pug is more chill than Piglet?

#PartyPooper
I'LL JUST REST MY EYES FOR A MINUTE.

#LeanOnMe
CAN SOMEONE HAND US THE REMOTE?

#TongueTied
DON'T MIND ME WHILE I DROOL FOR A WHILE.

#CuddlePuddle
FRIENDS MAKE THE BEST
PIG-LOWS.

#BedHogs
A LITTLE SNOUT SPACE,
PLEASE!

#HittingTheHay
THIS LITTLE PIGGY
NEEDED A NAP.

#BeachBums
RESTING UP BEFORE
WE HIT THE WAVES.

Hey! Time to Wake Up!

When he's not catching z's, Pug has a few tricks up his sleeve. He doesn't need more than a short walk every day, but he does enjoy a romp with his toys, and simple tricks are a piece of cake for him. To keep her mind sharp, Piglet is often spotted sniffing around, following the scent to adventure.

#KeepAway
IT'S MINE, IT'S MINE, IT'S **MINE!**

#ToyTrouble
A LITTLE HELP OVER HERE?

#PugPlaydate
LET'S BE BEST BUDS FOREVER!

#Squeal
SINGING IN THE MUD!

#FamilyDinners
NO HOGGING!

#NosetoNose
I "SCENTS" WE'LL
BE FRIENDS.

Best Accent

Old McDonald's pigs may have gone *oink*, but in other countries around the world, *oink* is lost in translation. And for that matter, so is *woof!* Find out what sounds other countries use for pigs and pugs and decide for yourself which ones sound best here, there, and everywhere!

Pugs

In the U.S., pugs go *woof, woof.* Maybe even *ruff, ruff.* But in Japan, people say their dog goes *wan wan.* In Sweden, they go *vov-vov.* And in Greece, they go *gav gav.* Sorry, Old McDonald, dogs don't go *E-I-E-I-O* in any language!

Piglets

There's no question what sound a pig makes in English: *oink!* And this Little Piggy definitely said "Wee, wee, wee!" when it squealed. In Dutch, however, pigs say *knor knor* and their squeals are *sweeks*. In Japanese, pigs say *boo boo*, and they squeal *bu-hii bu-hii* when they run all the way home!

Most Talented

By now we know that both Pug and Piglet have carved out their own special niche in this competition. But what if we put them both on a stage—or gave them their own reality show? Which would be named biggest show-off?

Pugs

Pugs are lovable and cuddle-able, but they can be superheroes, too! And some do amazing tricks, like skateboarding. One pug named Teddy (not pictured) became a social media sensation when his owner videotaped his bark, which distinctly sounded like he was saying "Batman!" His bark sent up the bat signal to pug lovers, who made mash-ups of Teddy's signature call and gained hundreds of thousands of views on YouTube. Holy Internet sensation, Pug!

Piglets

That's pretty hilarious, Pug. But Piglet will see your Batman and raise you a Picasso! Make that a PIGcasso! This sweet 450-pound (204-kg) domestic pig from South Africa has a very special talent: She paints! Put a paintbrush in Pigcasso's mouth, and she is in hog heaven! She stands in front of an easel and moves her head back and forth to create an abstract painting on canvas. When she's done, she signs her work by dipping her snout in paint and pressing it onto her finished work—her own stamp of approval.

47

Biggest Friend Magnet

After everything we've learned about Piglet and Pug, can we all agree that they would each make a pretty cool friend? They're smart, playful, athletic, helpful, and artistic. Anyone would want to hang out with these two, including some pretty unlikely critters!

Pugs

When two neighbors in the Philippines each got a new pet—a pug and a chick—they were a bit nervous to see what would happen when they introduced the unlikely duo. After all, a pug could easily overpower a little chick. But it turns out, the pair became instant besties! The puppy pug was curious yet gentle with the chick, and before long the chick followed him everywhere. These two hit it off so well they took to snoozing together, with the chick snuggled right under the pug's chin. The love was so real that the chick sometimes gave his puggy buddy a "peck" on the cheek.

Piglets

A pug and a chick are a charming duo, but how about a pig and a duck? There's not a lot in common there! Or is there? Hamlet, a potbellied pig that lives on a small farm in Kentucky, U.S.A., befriended Perry, a duck that joined the farmyard as a rescue. The pair sleeps and eats together, and the farm's owner says when they get separated Perry gets anxious and quacks for Hamlet until he finds him. What a quack up!

Most
Adventurous

Piglet and Pug, it's time to take a walk on the wild side. How about jumping out of an airplane? When pigs fly! Make that, when pugs fly! Or how about living on a deserted island in the middle of the Bahamas? Are you cocoNUTS? Let's see which one can bring the most extreme to this adventurous throwdown!

Piglets

No one knows exactly how a group of pigs ended up on Big Major Cay, an uninhabited island in the Bahamas—some say there may have been a shipwreck and the pigs on board swam ashore—but nevertheless, there are some semiferal pigs that live there, and they are living the tropical life. Tourists take day trips to pose for selfies with the pigs on the beach and even go for a dip in the ocean with them! #swimfriends!

Pugs

It's a bird! It's a plane! It's a ... pug?

That's right, a flying pug. In his youth, Otis, of California, U.S.A., completed 65 jumps while strapped to his owner's chest in a specially designed harness. He didn't have a cape, but he did wear "doggles"—goggles made especially for his puggy eyes!

Did you say ... doggles?

51

Best Sniffer

Besides their tails, Piglet's and Pug's snouts are probably their most distinct characteristic. Do you smell a winner yet?

Piglets

Piglet is sure putting her nose to the grindstone in this competition. And boy, is that snout talented! It may be leathery, but it is very sensitive. This is Piglet's specialized tool to search for and root out food. Pigs can detect odors in the air as many as seven miles (11 km) away and food buried 25 feet (8 m) underground! When it's not sniffing, that nose is digging, quickly moving dirt out of the way to uncover a snack.

Time-out for a fast fact:

IN EUROPE, PIGS WERE TRADITIONALLY USED TO LOCATE TRUFFLES, MUSHROOMS THAT GROW UNDERGROUND, ALTHOUGH THEY LIKE TO GOBBLE THEM UP ONCE THEY FIND THEM. THESE DAYS, DOGS USUALLY DO THE SNIFFING.

Pugs

Pug's nose has major *awww* factor. That squished, wrinkled sniffer is one of the defining characteristics of his silly mug. But it also brings a bit of trouble. Those nose wrinkles need to be cleaned often. And Pug's short snout isn't ideal for evaporating moisture, which can cause him to overheat easily. (The same is true for other flat-faced dogs, like bull-dogs, Boston terriers, and boxers.) Apparently, Pug's signature look comes with strings attached. That said, like pigs, dogs are excellent smellers. Their sense of smell is 1,000 times greater than that of humans. That's in part because of the structure of their noses and the fact that they have hundreds of millions more olfactory, or smell, receptors, which detect more airborne odor molecules, than we do.

Best Snack Buddy

Let's end this battle by pairing two things Piglet and Pug know a lot about: hanging out and having a snack. Of course, we humans want in on that fun. Would you rather share a cuppa with a pug or go on a picnic with a piglet?

Piglets

This little piggy went to a pignic. In 2015, London was host to a "micro pig pop-up," a five-day event during which you could visit newborn, pocket-size piglets, which adorably munched on carrot sticks and even dressed up in "wellies"—the British term for rain boots. Along with getting to play and cuddle with the piglets, guests were educated on something you now know: Pigs marketed as "teacup" or "micro" don't stay tiny—they grow up to be dog-size pets. Proper British piggy time paired with educated facts? Sounds like fun fit for the queen!

Pugs

Time to leave the royals and head to Japan for puggy teatime. Cat cafés and owl cafés have been trending for some time. Now it's time for something cutting edge: a pug café. That's right, for $5, you can sip on a beverage and spend an hour playing with a dozen or so curious pugs. Snuggle up on a rug with pugs and feed them treats? It's the ultimate pug playdate!

Time-out for a fast fact:
A CROSS BETWEEN A PUG AND A CHIHUAHUA IS CALLED A CHUG!

55

Decision Time

Wow, that was one intense battle!

Was it ever! Did you see that surfing pig? That came out of nowhere!

No kidding! And I never would have guessed Pug had ties to Dutch royalty! All hail, Pug!

Haha! Well, on that note, it's time to put a crown on the winner.

Indeed, it is. OK, kid! This is your big moment. You—and you alone—must choose the champion of this battle. In this ultimate throwdown, who has come out on top: PIGLET or PUG?

Piglets Replay
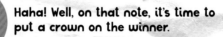

Weight: Up to 1,600 pounds (726 kg)
Smell skills: Detects odors 7 miles (11 km) away
History: Domesticated 9,000 years ago
Smarts: Excellent problem-solver
Superstition: Predicts bad weather
Trademark: Big ears, a big snout, and a loud oink
Eyesight: Poor
Sensitivity: Easily sunburns
Sleep: About 8 hours per day

Pugs Replay

Weight: On average 14–18 pounds (6–8 kg)
Smell skills: 1,000 times better than humans
History: Separated from wolves 40,000 years ago
Smarts: Can easily learn new tricks
Superstition: Omen of death
Trademark: Curly tail, big eyes, squishy nose
Eyesight: Excellent
Sensitivity: Sometimes gassy
Sleep: About 14 hours per day

Quiz: Are You a Piglet or a Pug?

You chose the winner, but there's one more piece of business that remains: Are YOU a pug or a piglet? Don't check for a curly tail, take this quiz to see if you're more piglet- or pug-like!

1 You have some downtime. You ...
A. go to a cool cafe and sip a smoothie.
B. head to the park for a picnic.

2 It's the weekend and you're headed outside. What's your go-to activity?
A. Ball sports
B. Water sports

3 Which of the following best describes you?
A. I'm up to date on the latest pop culture buzz.
B. I'm into classic TV shows and characters that I've known forever.

4 Who would you rather hang out with?
A. Rich and royals
B. Regular folks

5 Your friends say you are ...
A. quiet and not overly chatty.
B. one of the loudest people in the room.

6 On the weekends you prefer to ...
A. snooze till noon.
B. rise with the sun.

7 You finished your homework. What are you going to do next?
A. Sing some karaoke.
B. Pull out a canvas and make a painting.

8 You're feeling adventurous, so you ...
A. go skydiving.
B. go bodysurfing in the ocean.

If you mostly answered A, welcome to the club, Pug!

If you mostly answered B, you're on Team Piglet!

Next Up:
Explore More Pigs and Pugs!

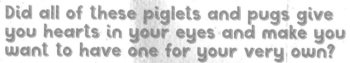

Did all of these piglets and pugs give you hearts in your eyes and make you want to have one for your very own?

Well, who could blame you?! But before you run and ask your mom or dad if you can have a new pet, there are a few things you should know. First of all, you've seen how adorable and fun pigs and pugs are, but they are also a lot of responsibility—maybe even more than some other pets—and require a lot of attention and care. In fact, not all cities even allow people to keep pigs as pets in their home. Neither pigs nor pugs are pets to quickly run out and bring home on a whim. Take your time, do some research with your parents, and really consider this commitment. If you do decide to bring home a new pet, consider rescuing one from a shelter. There are many pugs and pigs in shelters that need adopting. (Pigs especially are commonly brought to shelters because people don't realize how big they can get.) Check out these organizations to learn about pet adoptions in your area:

Best Friends Animal Society
bestfriends.org

The Humane Society of the United States
www.humanesociety.org

Pig Placement Network
www.pigplacementnetwork.org

Are you hungry to learn even more about pigs and pugs? Then chow down (or pig out!) on these resources to keep exploring!

Grab a parent and go online to check out these other resources.

WEBSITES

American Kennel Club: akc.org/dog-breeds/pug

American Mini Pig Association: americanminipig association.com

National Geographic Kids: kids.nationalgeographic .com/animals/pig

BOOKS

Maggitti, Phil. *Pugs: Complete Owner's Manual.* 2010

Rath, Sara. *The Complete Pig: An Entertaining History of Pigs.* 2011

Rice, Dan. *Pugs* (Barron's Dog Bibles). 2009

Thornton, Kim Campbell. *The Everything Pug Book: A Complete Guide to Raising, Training, and Caring for Your Pug.* 2005

Valentine, Priscilla. *Potbellied Pig Behavior and Training.* 2011

Index

Photo Credits

Illustrations throughout by Michael Byers.

Cover (pug), cynoclub/Shutterstock; (pig), Digital Zoo/Getty Images; back cover (LE), Stephen Marks/Getty Images; (RT), gp88/Shutterstock; back flap (UP), JStaley401/Shutterstock; (LO), Tsekhmister/Shutterstock; 2, Westend61/Getty Images; 3, fongleon356/Shutterstock; 4-5 (Background), tgavrano/Shutterstock; 4 (LE), Tsekhmister/Shutterstock; 4 (RT), Eric Isselee/Shutterstock; 8, Tsekhmister/Shutterstock; 8-9 (Background), jolly_photo/Shutterstock; 9, Africa Studio/Shutterstock; 11 (UP RT), Jevtic/iStockphoto/Getty Images; 11 (LO LE), Utekhina Anna/Shutterstock; 11 (LO RT), photomaster/Shutterstock; 11 (UP LE), HIP/Art Resource, NY; 12, Peter Muller/Getty Images; 13, o_sa/iStockphoto/Getty Images; 14, Fongleon356/iStockphoto/Getty Images; 15, S-F/Shutterstock; 16, Digital Zoo/Getty Images; 17, retales botijero/Getty Images; 18, Annette Shaff/Shutterstock; 19, RASimon/iStockphoto/Getty Images; 20, Ezzolo/Shutterstock; 20 (LE), DEA/G. Dagli Orti/De Agostini/Getty Images; 21, Peter Cripps/Alamy; 22, mauritius images GmbH/Alamy; 23, Jonn/Getty Images; 24, (c) Sue Chipperton; 25, W. Gilbert for WKC; 26, tirc83/Getty Images; 27, Annette Shaff/Shutterstock; 28 (CTR LE), Moviestore collection Ltd/Alamy; 28 (LO), AF archive/Alamy Stock Photo; 28 (UP LE), Norman Parkinson Archive/Getty Images; 28-29 (BACK), alphaspirit/Shutterstock; 28 (RT), photomaster/Shutterstock; 29, JStaley401/Shutterstock; 29 (UP RT), Kevin Mazur/Getty Images for Billboard; 29 (LO RT), Shirlaine Forrest/WireImage/Getty Images; 30, Byrdyak/iStockphoto/Getty Images; 31, Kristin Oldenburg/EyeEm/Getty Images; 32 (LO RT), Mur-Al/

iStockphoto/Getty Images; 32 (LE), HAP/Quirky China News/REX/Shutterstock; 32 (UP RT), Roger Wright/Getty Images; 33 (LO LE), Phillippe Diederich/Getty Images; 33 (LO RT), STR/NurPhoto via Getty Images; 33 (UP LE), Ezzolo/Shutterstock; 33 (UP RT), Ezzolo/Shutterstock; 34, Juniors Bildarchiv GmbH/Alamy; 35, blickwinkel/Alamy; 36, Daniel Grill/Getty Images; 37, Gandee Vasan/Getty Images; 38, Bruno Mathieu/Getty Images; 39, NotYourAverageBear/iStockphoto/Getty Images; 40 (LE), fongleon356/iStockphoto/Getty Images; 40 (UP RT), fongleon356/iStockphoto/Getty Images; 40 (LO RT), Africa Studio/Shutterstock; 41 (LO LE), Antony Nagelmann/Getty Images; 41 (UP LE), Hauke Dressler/LOOK-foto/Getty Images; 41 (UP RT), Jörg Mikus/EyeEm/Getty Images; 41 (UP RT), Buckeye Sailboat/Shutterstock; 42 (LO RT), Juniors Bildarchiv GmbH/Alamy; 42 (UP), Beate Zoellner/Getty Images; 42 (LO LE), Jojie Alcantara/Getty Images; 43 (LO), Johner Images/Getty Images; 43 (RT), Inti St Clair/Getty Images; 43 (UP), Janecat/Shutterstock; 44, Mark Liddell/Getty Images; 45, Lynn Stone/Getty Images; 46, Ezzolo/Shutterstock; 47, F.Schoenau/Caters News Agency; 48, Tim Ho/Caters News Agency; 49, Jeannie McAlpin; 50, BlueOrangeStudio/Alamy; 51, Sacramento Bee/ZUMA Press; 52, Erik Thor/Folio Images/Getty Images; 53, Beate Zoellner/Getty Images; 54, petpiggies; 55, Michael Nusair; 59 (UP LE), photomaster/Shutterstock; 59 (UP RT), Ermolaev Alexander/Shutterstock; 63, Eric Isselee/Shutterstock; 63, yevgeniy11/Shutterstock; 64 (UP LE), Lori Epstein/National Geographic Creative

You sure went whole hog, Piglet!

63

Bob Barker

For Bob Barker, who served as the inspiration for this book. —JB and the editors of Nat Geo Kids

Hot dog! That was a fun battle, Pug!

Published by National Geographic Partners, LLC. All rights reserved. Reproduction of the whole or any part of the contents without written permission from the publisher is prohibited.

Since 1888, the National Geographic Society has funded more than 12,000 research, exploration, and preservation projects around the world. The Society receives funds from National Geographic Partners, LLC, funded in part by your purchase. A portion of the proceeds from this book supports this vital work. To learn more, visit natgeo.com/info.

NATIONAL GEOGRAPHIC and Yellow Border Design are trademarks of the National Geographic Society, used under license.

For more information, visit nationalgeographic.com, call 1-800-647-5463, or write to the following address:

National Geographic Partners
1145 17th Street N.W.
Washington, D.C. 20036-4688 U.S.A.

Visit us online at nationalgeographic.com/books

For librarians and teachers: ngchildrensbooks.org

More for kids from National Geographic: natgeokids.com

National Geographic Kids magazine inspires children to explore their world with fun yet educational articles on animals, science, nature, and more. Using fresh storytelling and amazing photography, *Nat Geo Kids* shows kids ages 6 to 14 the fascinating truth about the world—and why they should care. kids.nationalgeographic.com/subscribe

For information about special discounts for bulk purchases, please contact National Geographic Books Special Sales: specialsales@natgeo.com

For rights or permissions inquiries, please contact National Geographic Books Subsidiary Rights: bookrights@natgeo.com

Designed by Amanda Larsen
Illustrations by Michael Byers

Hardcover ISBN: 978-1-4263-3176-3
Reinforced library binding ISBN: 978-1-4263-3177-0

The publisher wishes to acknowledge everyone who helped make this book possible: Ariane Szu-Tu, associate editor; Becky Baines, executive editor; Shannon Hibberd, senior photo editor; Christina Ascani, associate photo editor; Joan Gossett, editorial production manager; Anne LeongSon and Gus Tello, design production assistants; and Caitlin Holbrook and Doug Jeffery, for their creative input.

Printed in China
18/RRDH/1